Faithbuilders Bible Studies

The First Epistle of Saint Peter

WIPF & STOCK · Eugene, Oregon

by Mathew Bartlett & Derek Williams

Wipf and Stock Publishers
199 W 8th Ave, Suite 3
Eugene, OR 97401

The First Epistle of Saint Peter
By Bartlett, Mathew and Williams, Derek
Copyright©2019 Apostolos
ISBN 13: 978-1-5326-8096-0
Publication date 2/1/2019
Previously published by Apostolos, 2019

Cover Design by Blitz Media, Pontypool, Torfaen, UK.

Dedicated to all those who are hungry for God's Word.

More from Faithbuilders Bible Studies

Faithbuilders Bible Studies

The Faithbuilders Bible study series has been developed as a useful resource for today's students of God's Word and their busy lifestyles. Pastors, home or study group leaders and indeed for anyone wishing to study the Bible for themselves will benefit from using Faithbuilders studies.

Each volume is the result of many years of group Bible study, and has been revised in order to be relevant, challenging and faith building whilst remaining clear and easy to understand, helping more people to discover the blessings of God's Word.

Mathew Bartlett holds a Master's Degree in Biblical Studies from the University of Chester, England and is currently researching for a PhD in Greek rhetorical technique in Luke-Acts at the University of Roehampton, London. Derek Williams is a retired pastor and preacher with over 40 years of experience.

Contents

Introduction, Authorship and Date

Author, Date and Place of Writing

The author of this letter identifies himself as the apostle Peter (1:1). Simon was the fisherman from Galilee whom Jesus called to be his disciple and named him "Peter," "the rock." It is generally believed that he was writing around AD 62–63 during the reign of Nero. From 5:13 we may infer that Peter was writing from the place he calls "Babylon." For many commentators this is a coded reference to Rome (coded to hide his position from Roman authorities). Even so, recent discoveries by historians suggest that city life in urban Babylonia continued without pause from the time of Alexander until well into the Parthian period (150 BC to 226 AD). It is entirely possible that Peter's reference is to Mesopotamian Babylon, and that he is traveling there to preach among the diaspora (to whom he addresses the letter in 1:1). It should be recalled that Luke lists "Parthians" among those present on the day of Pentecost in Acts 2:9, which would readily explain Peter's links to the region.

The letter is addressed to diaspora Christians (possibly Christians who were converted from among the Jewish diaspora, or those Christians scattered by Judean persecution) who reside in "Pontus, Galatia, Cappadocia, Asia, and Bithynia." This area lies in modern Turkey, north of the Taurus Mountains, but at that time was under Roman rule.

The themes of the letter tend to confirm genuine Petrine authorship, for example, the author claims to be a witness of the crucifixion in 5:1 and (according to Eusebius) the letter was recognized as genuine from early times. It was ascribed to Peter by Irenaeus, Tertullian, Clement of Alexandria and Origen. The letter was probably also known by 1 Clement as early as AD 95, and certainly by Polycarp and the author of the Gospel of Truth (AD 140–150).

Some commentators have objected to Petrine authorship on the grounds that the Greek of the letter is of too high a quality to be ascribed to a Galilean fisherman. Yet this may be explained by the note in 5:12 that the apostle received help from Silas in writing the epistle. Similarly, claims that the persecution of Christians by Roman authorities implied by the letter came too late for Peter to know about are unfounded – it is well known that such persecution was already brewing in the days of Nero. That it is no earlier than AD 60, however, may be seen from the author's reference to Paul's letters to the churches. Traditionally, it is believed that Peter was executed during the reign of Nero around AD 67.

Purpose of Letter

The First Epistle of Peter has several major purposes. It contains clear statements of major Christian doctrines, so that the early church might have a record of the spirit and meaning of Christ's teaching from an authoritative source; Peter being one of the original twelve disciples. Secondly, it contains clear teaching for believers about how they ought to live surrendered, obedient and holy lives for Christ as they wait his return. Thirdly, it is written to believers who are facing persecution to encourage them to stand firm in the faith. The assurance Peter offers believers is that although they are called to follow Christ's example of suffering, they are just as certainly destined to join him in his eternal glory.

1 Peter 1

Themes in Chapter 1

The themes introduced in chapter 1 remain important throughout the letter. These themes deal with the practical realities being faced by the Christians at that time, as well as with spiritual teaching intended to help them through these difficulties.

To begin with, Peter introduces his readers as temporary residents, an allusion to their being pilgrims in the world. Pilgrimage is an image from the Old Testament Exodus, when God's people Israel were led out of slavery in Egypt to the promised land of Canaan where they would live as servants of God. Believers in Christ are pilgrims since they have left their former position as slaves to sin and Satan and have abandoned the lives they lived without Christ to journey with him towards a heavenly promised land.

When Israel left Egypt, it was not without the sacrifice and shedding of the blood of the Passover lamb. While Peter makes no explicit reference to the Passover as a festival, he understands the redemption of believers to have been accomplished through sacrifice – the shedding of the blood of Christ, a lamb without blemish and without spot (verse 19). This is a fulfilment of the OT description of the Passover lamb in Exod 12:5. In this context it is an allusion to Christ being without sin, which Peter states explicitly with a quote from Isa 53 in 2:22.

Indeed, the crucifixion is a major theme for Peter. As a witness of Christ's death and resurrection, Peter instructs his readers that Christ's suffering was ordained by God and foretold by the prophets (it is interesting to note the equivalence of verse 11 with Luke 24:26). The crucifixion was not an aberration, but central to God's plan before the earth was created (verse 20). It did not mean defeat for Christ but was the necessary precursor to the victory and everlasting glory of the resurrection. We have already noted that Peter's theology is informed by Isaiah 53, and although he does not quote this scripture until chapter 2 (verses 22–25), its influence is already felt in chapter 1, where Peter says the prophets spoke of the sufferings of Christ (verses 10–11).

Peter explains how Christ's suffering has not only brought glory to him, but immeasurable blessings for us who believe. When Peter speaks of moral and spiritual cleansing through the "sprinkling" of Christ's blood (verse 2), he is referring to what Jesus's death has accomplished for believers. These benefits also include our being born anew as God's children (verse 3), to an eternal, unchanging inheritance in heaven (verse 4), salvation (verse 5) and redemption (verses 18–19). Our faith has brought us great joy, which the troubles of life can never extinguish (verse 8–9).

Yet whilst Peter extols the benefits God has given to his children, he is realistic about their difficulties. He appreciates that believers face many and varied trials (verses 6–7). No one should be surprised if the followers of Jesus experience suffering as he did, for this is the way we must take. As we journey of our earthly pilgrimage from earth to heaven, the glory Christ has already entered on our behalf awaits us. The trials accomplish a good purpose in our lives: for when we stand the test it proves our faith to be genuine.

For Peter, the security of the believers is assured as they pass through trials, for God's word (his promise of salvation) is incorruptible and enduring (verse 23–25). Although Christians suffer, they are kept (preserved) through divine power (verse 5) until the coming of Christ. Indeed, the second coming of Christ is another major theme of the book, and in chapter 1, Peter sees it as heralding the end of all suffering for believers (verse 7). In the light of Christ's coming, Peter, recalling the words of Jesus (Mark 13:33), exhorts believers to be ready for action (verse 13), and to live holy lives as we await the final appraisal of Christ at his coming (verses 14–17).

Verse-by-Verse

Greetings

1:1 From Peter, an apostle of Jesus Christ, to those temporarily residing abroad (in Pontus, Galatia, Cappadocia, the province of Asia, and Bithynia) who are chosen.

The author of this letter is Peter, the fisherman, one of the twelve apostles that the risen Lord chose to be witnesses of his death and resurrection. Christ had given Peter the task of feeding his church (John 21:15–17). It is generally accepted that Peter was writing mainly to Jewish converts who had been scattered by persecution to the areas named. However, the letter is applicable to all Christians (see also 2 Pet 1:1).

Peter describes his Christian readers as "temporarily residing" ("pilgrims,") not only because many of them had left their homeland, but because just as Abraham was a temporary resident in Canaan, so all believers are temporary residents in the world (Heb 11:8–10, 13). This world is not our permanent home, we are just passing through it. Our home is in heaven (Phil 3:20).

1:2 According to the foreknowledge of God the Father by being set apart by the Spirit for obedience and for sprinkling with Jesus Christ's blood. May grace and peace be yours in full measure.

Before time began the eternal God, the Father, personally knew those who would hear the gospel message and receive Christ as their Saviour. He chose these to be his own. When we believed the gospel message we were set apart to God as by the work of regeneration the Holy Spirit baptized us into the body of Christ. We have become God's children in order that we might be obedient to Jesus Christ – *he is our Lord.* We who have believed know the power of the blood of Jesus Christ which cleanses us from all sin past, present and future (1 John 1:7) – *he is our Saviour.*

Peter's greeting is that the grace (undeserved favor of God) and true heart peace will be ours in increasing measure. Rather, since God's grace and peace are given us without measure, it is our experience and enjoyment of it that grows.

Praise God for Salvation

1:3 Blessed be the God and Father of our Lord Jesus Christ! By his great mercy he gave us new birth into a living hope through the resurrection of Jesus Christ from the dead.

Peter praises God, the Father of our Lord Jesus Christ, for his unlimited mercy in making us his children (1 John 3:1). We were guilty sinners deserving of hell, but now we are sons of God as the result of unlimited mercy. This was made possible by Christ's death and resurrection for us. Through faith in him we have been born again to a hope that is living and eternal. It is by Christ's resurrection that we have been raised to this exalted position, united with him.

1:4 That is, into an inheritance imperishable, undefiled, and unfading. It is reserved in heaven for you.

Since we are sons, we are also heirs of God (Rom 8:17). We have an inheritance – something that becomes our property when someone else dies. God's Son has already died to make this inheritance ours, and it is not corruptible like silver and gold, for it is not material but spiritual (Eph 1:3). It is not subject to impurity or decay and can never wear out. It is kept for us in a protected atmosphere – heaven itself. The individual is not reliant on self to keep their reward/inheritance – it is all in the hands of the eternal God. This is something for which we should be thankful as God who began the work of salvation in our lives will complete the work by bringing us to his eternal home (Phil 1:6).

1:5 who by God's power are protected through faith for a salvation ready to be revealed in the last time.

We, in turn, are kept (safeguarded) by God's power through faith, who will keep us until we receive that inheritance or "fully inherit that final salvation that is ready to be revealed at the last time." (AMPNT). The disciples of Christ are not dependent upon themselves to attain their full salvation but totally dependent upon the Lord.

The Trial of our Faith

1:6 This brings you great joy, although you may have to suffer for a short time in various trials.

We have every right to rejoice in our salvation even though at present we may be in "heaviness" as we pass through many kinds of trials. Our trials are hard and difficult. They distress us and weigh us down (Ps 34:19). The disciple of Jesus is not guaranteed a trouble-free life, however, they are, as Peter describes in this epistle, guaranteed God's help in those trials.

1:7 Such trials show the proven character of your faith, which is much more valuable than gold — gold that is tested by fire, even though it is passing away — and will bring praise and glory and honor when Jesus Christ is revealed.

God allows these trials for a reason. They are necessary to strengthen our faith. Since our faith is worth far more than gold, we should expect God to test it. Gold is tested or refined with fire to remove impurities. But our faith is tested by the trials that we go through so that it might increase and become strong. Gold does not last, but our faith will. God wants our faith to endure through the trials and difficulties of this life so that it might be proved genuine. This will result in praise, honor and glory being given to him who alone is the author and finisher of our faith (Heb 12:2).

1:8–9 You have not seen him, but you love him. You do not see him now but you believe in him, and so you rejoice with an indescribable and glorious joy. Because you are attaining the goal of your faith — the salvation of your souls.

Our faith revealed by the fact that although we have never seen Jesus Christ, yet we love him. Although we do not see him at this present time, we believe and fully put our trust in him (John 20:29). Our hearts are filled with joy in the present, the joy of our relationship with God, and yet this joy is one of anticipation, for one day we shall know him perfectly. Such a joy that cannot be expressed in words, for it is full of the glory of God, who is the source of our joy.

The outcome of our faith in Christ is the salvation of our souls, that is, the final deliverance from sin, its effects and its power.

The Coming of Christ Foretold

1:10–11 Concerning this salvation, the prophets who predicted the grace that would come to you searched and investigated carefully. They probed into what person or time the Spirit of Christ within them was indicating when he testified beforehand about the sufferings appointed for Christ and his subsequent glory.

The OT prophets foretold of the days when God's grace would be made available and pardon for sin offered to all. Although they spoke by the Holy Spirit of the sufferings of Christ and his subsequent glory (e.g. Isa 53), they did not fully understand what they said. They sought and asked of God carefully about this, wanting to find out more exactly the meaning of what was said and when it was going to happen.

1:12 They were shown that they were serving not themselves but you, in regard to the things now announced to you through those who proclaimed the gospel to you by the Holy Spirit sent from heaven — things angels long to catch a glimpse of.

In reply, God revealed to them that the message was not for them, nor for the time in which they lived. It was for a future day and would be revealed in fullness only when Christ came. We have now the fulfilment of the OT scriptures clearly shown in the Gospels. The facts concerning Christ are now made known to all men by the messengers whom he has sent, empowered by the Holy Spirit, to preach the gospel. Even the angels long to understand such precious and holy truth.

Instructions for Christian Living

1:13 Therefore, get your minds ready for action by being fully sober, and set your hope completely on the grace that will be brought to you when Jesus Christ is revealed.

In view of all that Peter has said so far we are to "gird up the loins of our mind" and be self-controlled, or "well-disciplined in spiritual matters" (my paraphrase). When a runner girds up his loins he is determined to continue and finish the race. So we are to be fully determined that we will continue in Christ in spite of difficulties. We are to set our hope fully on the grace that will be ours when Jesus Christ is revealed.

1:14 Like obedient children, do not comply with the evil urges you used to follow in your ignorance,

As we wait for the second coming of the Lord, our hope being fully set on his grace, we are to live as obedient children. We are not to let our lives be shaped by the sinful desires that ruled our lives before we came to know the Lord.

1:15–16 but, like the Holy One who called you, become holy yourselves in all of your conduct, for it is written, "You shall be holy, because I am holy."

Since we now know him, and he is holy, we are to be like him – holy in everything we do and say we are to be morally blameless and different to the world (Lev 11:44–45). Holiness is a theme which is lacking in many areas of the modern Christian church, but it remains a vital biblical principle that should be carefully observed.

1:17 And if you address as Father the one who impartially judges according to each one's work, live out the time of your temporary residence here in reverence.

We are among those who pray to God the Father, who judges every person according to their works and does not show favouritism. He will not condemn sin in an unbeliever and then condone it in a believer. So, whilst we are here on earth, we are to live in reverential fear and awe of God (1 Pet 2:17; Acts 9:31).

1:18–19 You know that from your empty way of life inherited from your ancestors you were ransomed — not by perishable things like silver or gold, but by precious blood like that of an unblemished and spotless lamb, namely Christ.

We must remember that we owe obedience as a debt to God because he has bought us with a high price—the precious blood of his Son Jesus Christ, who although he was without sin, gave himself for our sins on the cross. By his sacrifice we have been redeemed (bought back for God). We once lived empty, meaningless lives without God, just as our forefathers had done, in a way of life which they handed down to us. But now we have real meaning in our lives because we belong to God and share the life of his Son.

1:20 He was foreknown before the foundation of the world but was manifested in these last times for your sake.

Even before God had made the world, he saw the wrong choice man would make. It was God's plan to send his Son to be the Saviour of the world long before he made Adam. This plan was formed in eternity, foretold in the OT and fulfilled when Christ came.

1:21 Through him you now trust in God, who raised him from the dead and gave him glory, so that your faith and hope are in God.

When we heard the gospel message, we believed God, who raised his Son from the dead and glorified him, so that our faith and hope for salvation is not in God himself. To hear the gospel is to hear the personal voice of God to your soul (1 John 5:9; 1 Thess 2:13).

1:22 You have purified your souls by obeying the truth in order to show sincere mutual love. So love one another earnestly from a pure heart.

As Christians our souls have been purified by our obedience to the truth, that is our believing the gospel and trusting in Christ to save us. We have been born again and are cleansed by the word of God (Eph 5:26; Ps 119:9; John 15:3; 17:17). The evidence of this is that we also have a love for others who are also born of God (Jas 1:18; 1 John 5:1). We are to make sure that we continue to love our spiritual family fervently.

1:23 You have been born anew, not from perishable but from imperishable seed, through the living and enduring word of God.

We can do this now because our love is more than simply human. We are not born again of the corruptible seed of man; our natures have been changed. We are born by the eternal word of God whose nature is love (1 John 4:8).

1:24 For all flesh is like grass: and all its glory like the flower of the grass; the grass withers and the flower falls off,

Peter compares human nature to a flower or to grass, which withers and dies comparatively quickly. Dead or rotting flowers do not retain their beauty. So it is with the old nature. Man will die, and his honor and glory, power or fame will depart from him forever.

1:25 but the word of the Lord endures forever. And this is the word that was proclaimed to you.

But God's word will not pass away (Mark 13:31), and this is the word that we have heard through the gospel message. Hence our "new" nature (born of God's word) is contrasted with the old (corruptible). Due to the enduring nature of the word of God the disciple of Christ can rely on its content and promises and trust themselves to the salvation which God has described in its pages.

Discussion Questions for Chapter 1

1. In what way might Christians be described as strangers or pilgrims on the earth?

2. Make a list of all the things God has done for believers, as discussed in this chapter.

3. Why should believers take courage in the face of trials and difficulties?

4. In the light of Jesus's coming again, how should Christians live in this present world?

Going Deeper

Are Christians going to heaven? For Peter, the inheritance which God has made available for the believer is reserved in heaven (cf. Col 1:5). The earliest Christians understood heaven to be the place where God dwells (e.g. Mark 1:11; 6:41; 7:34; 8:11; 11:25 – Mark is believed to be the earliest gospel). Jesus had taught them not to lay up treasure on earth, but in heaven (Mark 10:21). Heaven is where Jesus is now (Mark 16:19; cf. Acts 7:55; Rom 10:6), the place from which he will soon return (Mark 14:62; 1 Thess 1:10). Believers are citizens of heaven (Phil 3:20) and the dead in Christ are currently in heaven (the implication of Eph 3:15, and the more explicit image of Rev 7:9–12).

In Phil 3:20–21, Paul tells us that the Lord Jesus Christ, in his resurrected body, is currently in heaven, and from there he will return and transform our bodies to be like his. The clear implication is that these bodies will, like his, be able to live in heaven. Furthermore, Paul insists in 1 Cor 15 that the flesh and blood bodies we currently inhabit cannot inherit "immortality" and "incorruption." These bodies must be replaced with spiritual ones that we may "inherit the kingdom of God" (15:50). Our bodies now bear the image of the earthly man (Adam) but will then bear the image of the heavenly man (Christ) (15:47).

Even so, Christian hope in the resurrection and eternal life was not based on our becoming spirits who fly around in heaven. Our resurrection bodies will be "spiritual" (15:46) and "heavenly" (15:49) and yet they are still "bodies." The resurrected Christ, as well as being able to live in heaven, remained on earth for a long period. He appeared to his apostles for 40 days (Acts 1:3) and ate and drank with them (Luke 24:39–42). And yet as the Gospel resurrection accounts show, Christ could appear and disappear at will (Luke 24:31). His body could be handled, and yet it could also seemingly pass through locked doors (John 20:19). Here was a resurrection which the early believers initially lacked precedent or vocabulary to explain. Even in John's first epistle, thinking of our resurrected bodies, we read: "what we will be has not yet been revealed." Yet John goes on to clarify "We know that whenever it is revealed we will be like him, because we will see him just as he is" (1 John 3:2).

The future of believers will certainly involve our spending time in "heaven," the immediate presence of God where Jesus is now. But other scriptures also indicate it will also encompass our living in the new heaven and the new earth, where God will dwell among us forever (Rev 21:1–4). It is not a case of either-or. It is a case of our being, in our incorruptible and immortal resurrection bodies, able to dwell with God eternally, and to live wherever God may be.

1 Peter 2

Themes in Chapter 2

Although Peter begins the chapter with exhortations for Christian living (2:1–5), he seems to divert into an exposition of the gospel and Christology (2:6–10) before returning to those exhortations (2:11–20), and once again to Christs suffering in 2:21–25. The reality for Peter is, of course, that the person and passion of Christ has brought believers to a privileged position, and that because of this privilege the believer also has certain responsibilities.

Consequently, Peter links his exhortation to humility with the humility of Christ. When calling believers to endure suffering with faith, he presents Christ as an example of patient suffering. He similarly bases his exhortation for Christians to lay aside malice and envy because we have, by God's grace, received the new birth and hence the nature of Christ, who was without malice.

When calling believers to live honestly and avoid worldliness, Peter's instructions are based on the idea that part of Christ's role is to make us a temple in which God dwells and in which we function as kings and priests to God. So if earlier exhortations are based on what Christ has done as an example, then the latter exhortations are based on what Christ has done and is doing in the believer's life.

Peter continues the theme of obedience to God's word. We accept Christ though the world rejects him. This acceptance of Christ brings us life and opens our eyes to the precious value of Christ. Through Jesus, we have a new sense of belonging, and responsibility, for we have become the people of God. We no longer live for sin but for the one who died for us and rose again. As we live in this world, awaiting the coming of Christ, we must behave decently and honestly, as lights in a dark place. This will silence our critics.

Throughout the letter Peter regards the crucifixion of Christ as of chief importance and, in the closing verses of this chapter, links his resurrection to his role as shepherd and overseer of each Christian soul (a theme he returns to in chapter 5).

Verse by Verse

Spiritual Babes

2:1–3 So get rid of all evil and all deceit and hypocrisy and envy and all slander. And yearn like newborn infants for pure, spiritual milk, so that by it you may grow up to salvation, if you have experienced the Lord's kindness.

Since we are: a) redeemed by the blood of Christ (1:19); b) born again of the Spirit, through faith in the word of God (1:23); and c) purified by that same Word (1:22); we are to put off the old nature, which was crucified with Christ and put on the new nature which is born of the Spirit. We are to lay aside all the misdeeds of our unregenerate nature. These are malice, which Lightfoot defines as a "vicious character generally." "Deceit" is falsehood which includes both telling lies and deliberately misleading people. "Hypocrisy" is pretense or insincerity. We are to let go of all grudges and ill feeling towards others ("envy"). We are to put off every kind of evil speaking, whether speaking evil of others ("slander"), or of God (blasphemy), and stop using bad language.

These things belong to our old nature. But since we are born again, we have become like spiritual infants, with a new nature. Just as babies crave their mother's milk, which helps them grow, so we are to crave the teachings of the word of God so that by it we may grow spiritually.

Thirsting for more of God should be the natural result of our being born again. Babies are always crying for more of their mother's milk. Why is that? It's because they have already tasted it and know it is good. Babies also know who they are receiving milk from, and the growing bond between mother and child is an important reason many women choose to breastfeed. In a similar way, as learn from God's word, we develop our relationship with him.

A Spiritual Temple, Spiritual Priests and Spiritual Sacrifices

A Spiritual Temple

2:4–5 So as you come to him, a living stone rejected by men but chosen and priceless in God's sight, you yourselves, as living stones, are built up as a spiritual house to be a holy priesthood and to offer spiritual sacrifices that are acceptable to God through Jesus Christ.

The Lord Jesus Christ was despised and rejected by men (Isa 53:3) but he is God's chosen one and is precious to him as his beloved Son (Matt 17:5). Rejection is a common theme in the life of Jesus. He faced rejection before his birth when there was no room in the inn, and the death threats of Herod against him as a child. In adult life he was rejected as being simply the carpenter's son. And of course, ultimately came the rejection which led to his crucifixion.

Peter is here referring to a major aspect of Christian living, the possibility of rejection due to the message we hold and the life we lead. However, the example of Jesus stands for every believer as they may experience rejection and suffering. Jesus is the only way of salvation, and we must come to him to be saved (Acts 4:12). Once we are saved, we must come to him to be built up in the faith.

Peter compares the church to a building. Christ is the living foundation of this building (see v. 6) and he is also its builder (Matt 16:18). Since we have received life from him, we too are living stones, being joined together as part of a place where God lives by his Spirit – this is the church (Eph 2:22). This is where God shall dwell for all eternity (Rev 21:3). Just as every stone in a wall supports others and is supported by others so it is in the church – we need each other.

Spiritual Priests and Spiritual Sacrifices

Not only are we the temple in which God dwells, Jesus Christ has made us a holy priesthood. As such we offer praise, worship and other spiritual sacrifices which are acceptable to God through Jesus Christ e.g. our bodies (Rom 12:1), thanksgiving (Heb 13:5), help given to others (Phil 4:18), and our Christian service (Phil 2:17).

The Rejected Stone

2:6–8 For it says in scripture, "Look, I lay in Zion a stone, a chosen and priceless cornerstone, and whoever believes in him will never be put to shame." So you who believe see his value, but for those who do not believe, the stone that the builders rejected has become the cornerstone, and a stumbling-stone and a rock to trip over. They stumble because they disobey the word, as they were destined to do.

Peter confirms his statement by quoting Isaiah 28:16. The chief cornerstone is the one that holds up the walls of a city or building – the foundation stone. The church's foundation is the Lord Jesus Christ, who was chosen by and is precious to God. No believer will be "disappointed," for whoever puts their trust in Christ will be eternally saved.

For the Christian, the Lord Jesus Christ is precious because we know that he loved us and shed his blood to cleanse us from sin. He saved our souls. But those who refuse to believe, and who reject the Lord Jesus Christ as their Saviour, will find him to be their judge. They will be condemned by their own rejection of him (John 3:18). Peter said in Acts 2:36 that God has made Jesus, who men rejected, Lord and Christ, the chief cornerstone. Although God has appointed him as a Saviour for all men, many refuse to believe and so remain in their sin. In this sense they stumble at him or the message of the gospel. He is the reason for their downfall, but only because they choose to reject him. God has made it clear in the scriptures what will happen to those who reject his Son (2 Thess 1:8–9).

A Chosen People

2:9–10 But you are a chosen race, a royal priesthood, a holy nation, a people of his own, so that you may proclaim the virtues of the one who called you out of darkness into his marvelous light. You once were not a people, but now you are God's people. You were shown no mercy, but now you have received mercy.

Those who receive Christ as Lord and Saviour are accepted by him. They become God's chosen people and are made a royal priesthood by Christ himself. Since we are a people set apart to God, we should be different from the world around us, for he has chosen us out of the world (John 15:19). We belong to God in a special way, since we have been redeemed by the death of his Son. We are his children, born of his Spirit. God has purposed, through us, to make known "the wonderful deeds and display the virtues and perfections of him Who has called you out of the darkness of sin into the most marvelous light of the knowledge of God." AMPNT.

Before we came to know Christ, we were not a people. Yes, we may have been part of a nation. Perhaps we are American, or perhaps we are Jews. But we were not all joined together as one people. But now, we have been constituted as the people of God, taken from every nation under heaven (Rev 5:9). As sinners we had not previously obtained mercy from God, till we came to Jesus Christ and found his mercy and forgiveness.

Peter takes his reference from Hosea 2:23, where the prophet promises that restoration is possible for the (at that time) backslidden nation of Israel. Peter is not alone among New Testament writers in expanding this idea— if backslidden Jews can be restored to be among God's people, then Gentiles too may be included if they repent and trust in Christ (see also Rom 9:24–26).

Instructions for Living as God's Chosen People.

2:11–12 Dear friends, I urge you as foreigners and exiles to keep away from fleshly desires that do battle against the soul, and maintain good conduct among the non-Christians, so that though they now malign you as wrongdoers, they may see your good deeds and glorify God when he appears.

God's people are only temporary residents on earth. Our true home is in heaven, and as heaven's citizens we should avoid the lusts of the flesh that constantly contend with our redeemed souls. Since we are servants of Christ, we are not to become slaves to sin. Peter is perhaps especially referring to sexual immorality which was as common in his day as it is today. Instead of living like the world around us, we must live honorably and honestly, so that although ignorant people speak evil of us as Christians, they may see our good deeds and glorify our Father in heaven (Matt 5:16).

2:13–15 Be subject to every human institution for the Lord's sake, whether to a king as supreme or to governors as those he commissions to punish wrongdoers and praise those who do good. For God wants you to silence the ignorance of foolish people by doing good.

We are Christ's representatives, like ambassadors in a foreign country, and so, for his sake, we must submit to every legal regulation of the country we live in. Submitting both to the supreme power of government and to those who receive their power from the government to maintain law and order (magistrates, police etc.). In this way we promote the gospel and stop the mouths of those who ignorantly oppose God.

2:16 Live as free people, not using your freedom as a pretext for evil, but as God's slaves.

We have been set free by Christ, but this freedom is not an excuse to do evil. Instead, we are to put our freed lives to use in the service of God. It is a great concern when people take the liberty of the gospel and abuse it by engaging in unholy living and sinful practices. All disciples should seek to live as Jesus commands and as the Holy Spirit enables. Be careful not to separate your life into two sections; i) my Christian experience that occurs on a Sunday and ii) my weekly 'normal' life which accepts an 'anything goes' mentality. Christ calls us to 24/7 Christianity; beware allowing the liberty of the gospel to turn into license.

2:17 Honor all people, love the family of believers, fear God, honor the king.

Christians should esteem all people, whatever their standing in life, giving them the respect that they deserve as human beings – for they are created in God's image. We are specially to love those who are our brothers and sisters in Christ. The fear of God Peter urges us to have is an awesome fear and reverence – not one that makes us afraid of God. Peter repeats his earlier charge to honor those in authority, such as kings, especially by paying our taxes. Christians should be model citizens, employers, employees, friends and neighbours to the glory of God.

At the end of this chapter and the beginning of the next Peter gives instructions to different groups of people so that each might know how to live his/her life as a pilgrim for God on the earth.

2:18–20 Slaves, be subject to your masters with all reverence, not only to those who are good and gentle, but also to those who are perverse. For this finds God's favor, if because of conscience toward God someone endures hardships in suffering unjustly. For what credit is it if you sin and are mistreated and endure it? But if you do good and suffer and so endure, this finds favor with God.

The Roman economy was built on slavery. Surprisingly, Peter does not call for all slaves to be set free. It is not that he thought slavery was good. Rather, Peter was ministering to God's people *where they were*, and we must do the same. As he urges them to serve their masters well, even if they are wicked men who dish out unfair punishments, he is calling them to follow the example of Christ, who suffered a slave's death so that he might give us, and them, spiritual freedom.

This is how slavery eventually ended. First, people found spiritual freedom in Christ, and their faith led them to peacefully oppose slavery in all its forms. Peter is not excusing the evil of slave masters but demonstrating that it is not with carnal but spiritual weapons that evil can be defeated.

2:21 For to this you were called, since Christ also suffered for you, leaving an example for you to follow in his steps. He committed no sin nor was deceit found in his mouth. When he was maligned, he did not answer back; when he suffered, he threatened no retaliation, but committed himself to God who judges justly.

Christ's example stands out above all, and as Christians we have been appointed to follow him in suffering and trouble. Christ never did anything wrong and never spoke an untrue word. Yet they beat him, spat on him, and nailed him to a cross. When they spoke all kinds of evil against him, he did not retaliate. When he was abused, he made no threats of vengeance. Instead, he entrusted himself and his rights to his Father, whom he knew would render justice in due time. In all this he has set us an example that we might react to unjust suffering in the way that he did.

2:24 He himself bore our sins in his body on the tree, that we may cease from sinning and live for righteousness. By his wounds you were healed.

Jesus Christ took our sins in his own body on the cross. This is a clear statement of the atoning nature of Christ's death. In the words of Saint Paul, "God made the one who did not know sin to be sin for us, so that in him we would become the righteousness of God" (2 Cor 5:21). As Jesus died, our sinful natures are reckoned by God to have died with him. Now he lives again so that we might share his risen nature and live for God and righteousness. The sufferings that Christ bore for us are sufficient to heal our whole being – body, soul, and spirit – for eternity.

2:25 For you were going astray like sheep but now you have turned back to the shepherd and guardian of your souls.

We had wandered far from God like lost sheep (Isa 53:6), but through his cross, Christ has brought us back to himself. We have returned to the shepherd and guardian of our souls (Heb 13:20).

Discussion Questions for Chapter 2

1. What does Peter mean when he says that since we are born again, we should desire the sincere milk of the word which will enable us to grow?

2. In what ways have believers become spiritual temples, and spiritual priests making spiritual sacrifices?

3. In what ways can Christians prove that God has called them "out of darkness into his marvellous light?"

4. How do Peter's words about Christ's suffering at the end of this chapter remind us of Isaiah 53?

Going Deeper

Peter's theology of the cross is clearly informed by Isaiah 53, which is quoted in this chapter, and alluded to throughout the letter.

> He is despised and rejected by men,
> A Man of sorrows and acquainted with grief.
> And we hid, as it were, *our* faces from him;
> He was despised, and we did not esteem him. (Isaiah 53:3)

Peter may well have this verse in mind when he refers to the rejection of Jesus Christ by unconverted men in 2:4. He links this theme with another passage (Ps 118:22), which predicts Christ's rejection by Israel's rulers and pronounces their consequent condemnation. Peter broadens the meaning of the Psalm to encompass all who reject Christ ("those who do not believe" – 2:7). The stumbling of those who do not believe is both foretold and foreordained (2:8). Yet it is important to note that this does not necessarily indicate that God has arbitrarily foreordained that certain individuals would be Christ rejecters. It may be more correct to suppose that Peter means that just as God had foreordained and foretold that those who receive Christ would be saved, so God has made clear through his prophets that those who reject Christ would be destined for judgment. This interpretation is useful since it allows God alone to remain as the sovereign author of salvation, without precluding the idea of human responsibility.

1 Peter 3

Themes in Chapter 3

Peter continues to give instructions about Christian relationships. Having dealt with slaves and masters, he now turns to husbands and wives. Yet as in chapter 2, for Peter these practical matters are also devotional, in the sense that they are based on Christ's own teaching, and observance of them results in God being glorified.

It is also interesting to note that Peter's instructions to women centre on the evangelistic activity of Christian women winning their own husbands for Jesus. For Peter, whom Christ called to be a "fisher of men" (Matt 4:19) the presentation of the gospel is at the heart of everything. Peter's attitude concerning the place of husbands and wives in the family appears traditional and patriarchal, until one factors in his astonishing statement that both are "fellow heirs of the grace of life." Peter does not seek to upset prevailing conventions himself, he recognizes that in Christ something new and revolutionary has already begun, the equivalent of Paul's eschatological view that "there is neither male nor female" in Christ (Gal). For Peter this balance between the present and the coming worldviews is what brings peace to the home life; as does his call for believers to live in harmony with sympathy, affection, forbearance, forgiveness, and humility.

Peter realizes that the present world is out of accord with God's plan and purposes, and that this enmity against God will be manifest in people's enmity against the believing people of God. The result will eb persecution, opposition and suffering for believers in the present age. And yet this should not surprise us, for it was the reaction of the world to Christ his Son, who through his suffering has set us an example. Like Christ, we are to suffer persecution faithfully and patiently, committing our souls to God and trusting him to put all things right on the Day of Judgment.

Yet Peter concludes the chapter with what is almost a doxology, praising what God had accomplished through the suffering of Christ in saving our souls and cleansing us from sin. As always, for Peter

Jesus is the centre of this outburst of worship, and worthy of the exaltation which followed his suffering: "Jesus Christ ... went into heaven and is at the right hand of God with angels and authorities and powers subject to him."

In a similar way, readers might infer that since Christ's victory is so complete, their sharing in his suffering will be followed by sharing in the eternal blessings he has obtained on their behalf.

Vere by Verse

Relationships at Home

3:1–2 In the same way, wives, be subject to your own husbands. Then, even if some are disobedient to the word, they will be won over without a word by the way you live, when they see your pure and reverent conduct.

At first glance, the instruction that a wife must be submissive to her husband may seem, at the very least, out of date. However, when we examine the verses in context, we will find some enduring principles which still apply today.

The Amplified NT reads that the wife is to: "subordinate herself as being secondary to and dependent upon him and adapt herself to him." This instruction corresponds with the general teaching by Jesus that his disciples are to be humble and submissive to each other. In doing so, they are following the example of Christ, who is meek and lowly in heart (Matt 11:28–30). Wives who live in this way as Christ commands may be able to win their husbands for Jesus, even without a word being spoken. The husband may be won over as he sees the purity, modesty, and reverence for God in his wife's new life. Some translations regard the wife's reverence to be for her husband. The Amplified NT has that the wife is to respect, defer to and revere, which is, to honor, esteem, appreciate, prize and in the human sense adore (i.e. admire praise, be devoted to, deeply love and enjoy your husband).

3:3–4 Let your beauty not be external — the braiding of hair and wearing of gold jewelry or fine clothes — but the inner person of the heart, the lasting beauty of a gentle and tranquil spirit, which is precious in God's sight.

A godly woman (although this is especially written to wives it applies to all women) should not adorn herself with a beauty that is merely outward and passing, the kind which is produced by the braiding of one's hair or the wearing of jewelry or expensive clothes. Instead, she should cultivate a gentle and (submissive) quiet spirit, which has a beauty that will never pass away, and which is precious in God's sight, because it is in the likeness of his Son (see 2 Cor 10:1).

3:5–6 For in the same way the holy women who hoped in God long ago adorned themselves by being subject to their husbands, like Sarah who obeyed Abraham, calling him lord. You become her children when you do what is good and have no fear in doing so.

The way to live a godly life has not changed. The holy women of the OT were clothed with holiness and strong in faith, and yet were submissive to their own husbands. These strong women of faith are examples to Christian women today.

Sarah is perhaps the example who outshines them all, and yet she acknowledged the authority of her husband Abraham, submitting to him and obeying him. When Peter says that all who follow her example will be her true daughters. Yet he urges them always to do right without giving way to hysterical fear, letting anxiety unnerve them. Obviously, Peter does not equate submissiveness with weakness. The woman of God, through faith, is to stay strong (with God's strength) for her family.

3:7 Husbands, in the same way, treat your wives with consideration as the weaker partners and show them honor as fellow heirs of the grace of life. In this way nothing will hinder your prayers.

Speaking as a married man, Peter may well have considered his wife to be the weaker partner. Yet he urges husbands to be considerate of their wives, recognizing and making allowances for their weaknesses. Husbands must acknowledge their wives to be equal sharers in the grace of life, that is, in salvation. We are all equal at the foot of the cross, since we owe all to the One who died for us. If the husband does not keep this fact in mind and act accordingly then his prayers will not be answered.

Relationships in the Church

3:8–12 Finally, all of you be harmonious, sympathetic, affectionate, compassionate, and humble. Do not return evil for evil or insult for insult, but instead bless others because you were called to inherit a blessing. For the one who wants to love life and see good days must keep his tongue from evil and his lips from uttering deceit. And he must turn away from evil and do good; he must seek peace and pursue it. For the eyes of the Lord are upon the righteous and his ears are open to their prayer. But the Lord's face is against those who do evil.

Having spoken to husbands and wives, Peter, still talking about relationships, addresses "all of you." He tells us how we ought to behave toward the church of God, our brothers and sisters in Christ.

> We are to be united in spirit (one mind).

> We are to show compassion, sympathizing with one another.

> We are to love each other as those who are born of the same Spirit and who have the same Father.

> We are not to be hard hearted to each other, but tender-hearted. This means we will be open and vulnerable.

> We are to be humble minded and always polite.

> We are not to do evil in repayment for evil done to us (especially in the church).

> We are not to return insult for insult, but we are to bless and to seek the benefit of the one that has insulted or wronged us. Pray for them and love them. By God's grace we will overcome, and as we prove ourselves to be his children, will receive his blessing (Matt 5:44–45).

Peter quotes Psalm 34:12–16. Anyone who wants to enjoy a good and long life filled with God's blessing must act and speak in a way that pleases God. He must not lie, curse or speak evil of others (is Peter remembering his own failure and later repentance here? Matt 26:74). Only the repentant sinner who turns from wrong to do good, eagerly following God's way in peace with God will experience God's protection and answers to their prayers, for God sternly opposes all who do evil.

Suffering as Christians in a Sinful World

3:13–17 For who is going to harm you if you are devoted to what is good? But in fact, if you happen to suffer for doing what is right, you are blessed. But do not be terrified of them or be shaken. But set Christ apart as Lord in your hearts and always be ready to give an answer to anyone who asks about the hope you possess. Yet do it with courtesy and respect, keeping a good conscience, so that those who slander your good conduct in Christ may be put to shame when they accuse you. For it is better to suffer for doing good, if God wills it, than for doing evil.

Is there anyone that will harm us if we are eager to do good? Who has the right to do so? Even if we are harmed or threatened by men we can leave the matter in God's hands. He sees that we do right, and he is the judge. When we suffer for doing right, we will be blessed in accordance with what Christ said (Matt 5:10–12). We are not to fear those who abuse us nor be anxious about what they threaten to do.

Instead, we are to make up our minds to still obey Jesus as Lord, in spite of any opposition this may bring. We must always be ready to give a simple and clear answer to those who ask the reason for our hope of eternal life with courtesy and respect. By doing this we will keep a clear conscience so that when we are falsely accused; those who threaten us abusively and revile our right behavior in Christ may come to be ashamed (of slandering our good lives) (see AMPNT).

Suffering persecution because we are living for God may be tough, but Peter insists that it is better to suffer wrongfully for doing right than to suffer justly for doing wrong.

Christ our Example and Saviour

3:18 Because Christ also suffered once for sins, the just for the unjust, to bring you to God, by being put to death in the flesh but by being made alive in the spirit.

Peter again points to Christ as our example. He never did anything wrong, yet he suffered. He was the only perfectly righteous one, yet he gave up his life to reconcile us, unrighteous people, to God. He died, but after three days was raised to life again by the Holy Spirit.

3:19–20 In it he went and preached to the spirits in prison, after they were disobedient long ago when God patiently waited in the days of Noah as an ark was being constructed. In the ark a few, that is eight souls, were delivered through water.

It was by the power of the Holy Spirit that, during the three days that Christ's body lay in the tomb, his spirit descended into Hades (the place where the spirits of the dead are, both righteous and unrighteous) and preached the gospel to those who were there. Among these, says Peter, were those who had disobeyed God in the days before the flood. Although God had warned Noah that he would destroy the world because of human wickedness, most people did not believe Noah's warnings, and only eight persons were saved in the ark. As discussed in "Going Deeper" section of this chapter, it is not my view that Peter believes these disobedient sinners were saved through the news of Christ's victory over death. Rather, it is my view that the news of Christ's victory which brought deliverance to the righteous in Hades who waited for God's salvation, also brought news of final condemnation for the ungodly.

3:21–22 And this prefigured baptism, which now saves you — not the washing off of physical dirt but the pledge of a good conscience to God — through the resurrection of Jesus Christ, who went into heaven and is at the right hand of God with angels and authorities and powers subject to him.

The flood is a picture to us of water baptism, which is not a means of our being washed physically clean, but which identifies us with the death and resurrection of Christ. By raising Christ from the dead, God has raised us too. He has given witness to the fact that Christ's death is sufficient ground for our salvation. It is by our faith in him that we are justified – that is, our sins have been forgiven and we have a clear conscience before God.

Christ having been raised from the dead has gone into heaven and has sat down at the right hand of God, having been given absolute power and authority over all created things, whether visible or invisible.

The idea of sitting down at the right hand of God has two connotations. Firstly, the priests making offerings would always stand and repeatedly make them. That Christ has sat down is an indication that he will never need to repeat his sacrifice. It is enough once for all (Heb 10:1112). Secondly, it is the position of power and authority. Those Christ saves are secure in that salvation, for there is no power greater which can pluck them out of his hand (John 10:28).

Discussion Questions for Chapter 3

1. How do you think a Christian woman can be submissive to her husband and yet be strong in faith?

2. In what practical ways can a husband how consideration for his wife without regarding her as inferior?

3. Think of what Peter says in vv. 8–12. How might these verses be worked out for you in your local church life?

4. Why are Christians called to suffer?

Going Deeper

Peter's discussion of Christ's descent into Hades and his preaching to the spirits in prison has attracted a wide variety of interpretations down through the centuries. These range from the spirit of Christ, in Noah, preaching the gospel to the disobedient before the flood (Augustine's view) to Christ preaching salvation to recover the lost in Hades, to his preaching his final triumph over death, in a way which left the unrepentant still in condemnation.

In this study guide, I have discussed the most straightforward explanation, as I see it, which suggests itself from the text. As discussed in the "Verse by Verse" section, this explanation involves Christ's spirit, after his death but before this resurrection, being precisely where he told the thief on the cross he would be that same day—"today" (after his death) "you will be with me in paradise" (Luke 23:43). Since it is evident that Christ's spirit was absent from his body for three days until the resurrection, once may reasonably assume that Christ was in "Paradise" for these three days.

Some confusion arises when Christian believers read "heaven" for "paradise." In the account of the rich man and Lazarus given in Luke 16:19–31, the beggar Lazarus was carried after death by the angels to "Abraham's bosom"– a resting place and a paradise but not heaven. This place of the dead (Hades) was believed by Jews and Greeks alike to be somewhere in the heart of the earth and divided into two sections—a place of paradise and a place of punishment, with a great uncrossable gulf fixed between.

Due to the lack of support in scripture for the view that post-mortem salvation is possible for the ungodly, it is unlikely that Peter is thinking of this. Indeed, Jesus's words in Luke seems to preclude this—for when the rich man cried out for mercy from the fire of Hades, none was offered (Luke 16:24–26). Indeed, the text, "if they do not listen to Moses, they will not be persuaded though one rise from the dead" (Luke 16:31) may suggest even news of Christ's victory over death would not be enough to save unrepentant sinners post-mortem. Rather, it was believed that the faithful, those who worshipped God prior to Christ's coming, were in the paradise section of Hades, and that Christ went there with good news that now they could follow him into the presence of God as he took them with him at his ascension to heaven; which some assume may be the background to Ephesians 4:8–10:

> Therefore it says, *"When he ascended on high he captured captives; he gave gifts to men."* Now what is the meaning of *"he ascended,"* except that he also descended to the lower regions, namely, the earth? He, the very one who descended, is also the one who ascended above all the heavens, in order to fill all things.

Peter's reference to Christ's preaching to the disobedient would then convey the meaning that the gospel which announced deliverance to the faithful also brought news of final doom to the unfaithful. After all, Peter's focus is on Christ's universal announcement of the gospel, his victory over death, rather than the response of the hearers.

It would be a brave man indeed who would stake his claim to be right about this subject, with a theology based on a single, obscure verse! But that does not mean that we can dodge the issue. What the reader can be assured of, however, without controversy, is that Jesus Christ has overcome death, and in his name the message of hope and eternal life is now being announce to all people.

1 Peter 4

Themes in Chapter 4

In this chapter, Peter calls believers to leave behind the sinful excesses of their past lives and fully commit to following Jesus Christ. Such commitment to Christ and separation from the world is bound to lead to opposition from the unconverted. As we face this opposition, we are following in the footsteps of Jesus, and should remain focused on him as our example. We are to be so committed to Christ that not even suffering, opposition or persecution will turn us away from being faithful to God. In this way we commit ourselves to God's keeping regardless of circumstances, because we are assured of ultimate and eternal victory.

Although Peter is very conscious that the end of the present world was imminent, and even though he exhorts believers to holiness of life and separation from worldly lusts, he does not advocate any kind of religious escapism. Instead, his thoughts about the coming judgment lead him to very practical real-world exhortations. Believers are to be self-controlled, hospitable, serving each other in love. They are also to be steadfast in prayer, for in the light of Christ's near return, Peter exhorts us to be watchful and take our commitment to prayer seriously.

In every area of life, the beleiver is motivated to live for the glory of God, since the only approval that counts comes from God.

Verse by Verse

Living for God's Will

4:1–2 So, since Christ suffered in the flesh, you also arm yourselves with the same attitude, because the one who has suffered in the flesh has finished with sin, in that he spends the rest of his time on earth concerned about the will of God and not human desires.

Believers are no longer of the world, for Christ has chosen us out of the world (John 15:19). As a result, we can expect to experience trouble and suffering just as he did (John 16:33). Christ died for our sins (1 Cor 15:3) and in him we have died to sin (Rom 6:2; 6:6). So we are to reckon ourselves dead to sin, no longer obeying it and giving in to its desires (Rom 6:11–12). Christians face an ongoing battle with sin, from within (sinful attitudes/temptation) and without (the opposition of sinful people – Heb 12:3). We must "arm ourselves" or "prepare" our minds to face such sufferings as the lot of every Christian. By so doing we are following in the example of him who gave his life for us.

Jesus always sought to do God's will, and since we have died with Christ, and now live together with him, possessing a new nature that is born of God, we too should delight to do God's will.

4:3–5 For the time that has passed was sufficient for you to do what the non-Christians desire. You lived then in debauchery, evil desires, drunkenness, carousing, drinking bouts, and wanton idolatries. So they are astonished when you do not rush with them into the same flood of wickedness, and they vilify you. They will face a reckoning before Jesus Christ who stands ready to judge the living and the dead.

Peter's description of a life lived without God being filled with drinking parties and casual sex looks as much like the 21st century as it does the 1st century. Idolatry may be less of a vice in the West but is still endemic in many cultures. "Enough of all this!" cries Peter. We have left all this behind to follow Jesus.

Unbelievers, especially our former friends, are unable to understand what has happened to us. An unsaved person cannot understand what it means to be "born again", they just think it strange that our way of life has changed. They think we've gone weird or "got religion" and they heap abuse on us.

But they shall have to give an account to God for this abuse and for the way they live. God, says Peter, is ready to judge all people, both the living (saved) and the dead (unsaved).

4:6 Now it was for this very purpose that the gospel was preached to those who are now dead, so that though they were judged in the flesh by human standards they may live spiritually by God's standards.

This verse is notoriously difficult to understand. J. B. Phillips helpfully paraphrases it, by understanding "dead" to refer to those outside of Christ: "For that is why the dead also had the Gospel preached to them—that it might judge the lives they lived as men and give them also the opportunity to share the eternal life of God in the spirit."

4:7–8 For the culmination of all things is near. So be self-controlled and sober-minded for the sake of prayer. Above all keep your love for one another fervent, because love covers a multitude of sins.

Peter has already revealed that he saw the end of the age (and with it, the coming of Jesus) as imminent, and as a motivation for holy living. Since there will be a day of judgement, we should be serious, self-controlled and always stay alert to our need of disciplined prayer. More than anything else, as the day of Christ approaches, we must love one another fervently (intensely and unfailingly) for love forgives and disregards the offences of others (Prov 10.12).

Serving in God's Will

4:9–10 Show hospitality to one another without complaining. Just as each one has received a gift, use it to serve one another as good stewards of the varied grace of God.

As Christ has entrusted us with his gifts, which differ for everyone. We are to be good stewards of what he has given by using those gifts for his interests, building up his church. Whatever we have received we are to minister one to another.

Peter puts hospitality at the top of his list. As Christians we must offer hospitality to other Christians and help to provide for their needs in terms of lodging, feeding, clothing or giving them whatever else they need. We are to do this without grudging the cost or time spent or the giving of ourselves.

4:11 Whoever speaks, let it be with God's words. Whoever serves, do so with the strength that God supplies, so that in everything God will be glorified through Jesus Christ. To him belong the glory and the power forever and ever. Amen.

It is important for those who teach God's church that they should only teach according to the word of God, making his will and counsel known. Anyone who serves in more practical ways should do so with the strength that God provides. Peter understands Christian service to bring praise and glory to God, who after all is entirely worthy of this praise! Clearly for Peter, the glory of God is the Christian's motivation in service.

Suffering in the Will of God

4:12–13 Dear friends, do not be astonished that a trial by fire is occurring among you, as though something strange were happening to you. But rejoice in the degree that you have shared in the sufferings of Christ, so that when his glory is revealed you may also rejoice and be glad.

As believers we should never be bewildered about the sufferings we encounter, which Peter calls a "trial by fire." The picture Peter gives is of gold being refined in a furnace. The fire does not destroy the gold – it purifies it. When trouble comes into our lives, threatening to destroy us, we need not fear, for it cannot destroy us. Instead, God permits these trials to strengthen our faith. We should not regard the trial as something that should not be happening to us. We all know the expressions "Why me?" "It's not fair!" or "You can't do this to me!" We might be tempted to think that because of who we are, God's people, we are immune from suffering.

For Peter, the explanation for why Christians suffer is that we are being given the privilege of sharing in Christ's experience of suffering; so rather than complaining, we should rejoice! Although Jesus suffered, He has now entered his glory (Luke 24:26). In the same way, since we now share in his sufferings, we will share in his glory with tremendous joy when he comes again (2 Tim 2:12).

4:14 If you are insulted for the name of Christ, you are blessed, because the Spirit of glory, who is the Spirit of God, rests on you.

Peter here reminds us of the teaching of Jesus in Matt 5:11–12. As people revile and insult us, it is not us they are really insulting, but the Spirit of Christ in us. Whilst he is insulted by them, he is glorified by our obedience to the truth which is proof of God's grace in our lives.

4:15–17 But let none of you suffer as a murderer or thief or criminal or as a troublemaker. But if you suffer as a Christian, do not be ashamed, but glorify God that you bear such a name. For it is time for judgment to begin, starting with the house of God. And if it starts with us, what will be the fate of those who are disobedient to the gospel of God?

We must never be ashamed when we suffer for Christ (2 Tim 1:11–12). However, Peter makes clear that when he speaks of suffering for Christ, he means unjust suffering. The suffering of punishment by murderers, thieves or any other kind of criminal is just, and we should not be among them. We should not even be those who are reproached for meddling in the private affairs of others. Neither doing wrong, nor suffering for doing wrong, will bring any glory to God. As those who bear Christ's name ("*Christ*ians") we must not bring shame on his name but are to live to glorify God.

Another aspect of Christian suffering is introduced by Peter in verse 17. God is our heavenly father. He corrects and disciplines us. Often this discipline will take the form of suffering. Such discipline is not punitive; that is, it is not to punish us for doing wrong, but rather to teach us to do right. We should be thankful for it (Heb 12:5–11). God, who is holy, will deal with his children with stern discipline. Yet the discipline that believers experience is only for a time (1 Cor 11:32), in this life, as God trains us to be his children. Unbelievers are not his children, and so he is unable to correct them. Instead, God will deal with unbelievers as a judge and the punishment will be punitive and everlasting (Rev 20:15).

4:18 And if the righteous are barely saved, what will become of the ungodly and sinners?

This quote of Prov 11:31 is, on the face of it, incorrect. No one is "scarcely" saved, for Jesus Christ saves to the uttermost. The question is rhetorical. What Peter means is that if God deals with his children so strictly, how much worse will be the punishment that the wicked and ungodly can expect to receive from him?

4:19 So then let those who suffer according to the will of God entrust their souls to a faithful Creator as they do good.

Since we have learned that the trials of life are intended by God for our good (Rom 8:28), let us take encouragement and place ourselves in the hands of him who does all things well. Let us commit the keeping of our souls to him, who is faithful to his promise and continue to do good, surrendering our lives unreservedly to him (2 Tim 1:12).

Discussion Questions for Chapter 4

1. In what ways can believers arm themselves with Christ's mind as they face trials and suffering?

2. Why do unbelievers react negatively to our change of lifestyle?

3. List several reasons why as Christians we should use our gifts to serve each other.

4. Why can Christians rejoice when they face various kinds of suffering?

Going Deeper

Every Christian will experience suffering at some time or another (Acts 14:22), but our suffering is never without purpose. There are many kinds of suffering in life. Peter focuses on the persecution of Christians, which no doubt was the reality which faced his first readers. However, there are many other forms of trial which believers face these can be physical, mental, and spiritual trials.

One of the reasons we face persecution is that we are no longer of this world. Christ's call to follow him is a call to live counter-culturally in this present age. Peter touches lightly on this subject when he says that we are no longer to live in sinful excess as the world does, but perhaps he had in mind the words of Jesus, "If you belonged to the world, the world would love you as its own. However, because you do not belong to the world, but I chose you out of the world, for this reason the world hates you" (John 15:19).

The world hates us because it first hated the Christ whom we represent (John 15:18). We are all together in this, which is why Peter calls believers to support and serve each other in love. Paul says much the same in Galatians 6:2 when he writes, "Carry one another's burdens, and in this way you will fulfill the law of Christ." Those who have suffered are able to help and encourage others as they pass through similar sufferings (2 Cor 1:4). Many of us are grateful for the times, when we have been faced with problems, that God's people have come alongside us to offer help and support.

For Christians, suffering produces many spiritual benefits, which Peter highlights in chapter 1:7. The trial of our faith produces character (a subject he will enlarge on in his second letter (2 Peter 1:5–8). Paul also expounds on the benefits of suffering, since "suffering produces endurance, and endurance, character, and character, hope." (Romans 5:3–4). If the believer endures suffering in Christ's name, and by following Christ's example, then Peter says he or she will be blessed:

> If you are insulted for the name of Christ, you are blessed, because the Spirit of glory, who is *the Spirit of God, rests* on you. (1 Peter 4:14)

> Do not return evil for evil or insult for insult, but instead bless others because you were called to inherit a blessing. (1 Peter 3:9)

Again, Peter, who all the gospels agree was close to Jesus, may have Christs own words in mind here:

> Blessed are you when people insult you and persecute you and say all kinds of evil things about you falsely on account of me. Rejoice and be glad because your reward is great in heaven, for they persecuted the prophets before you in the same way. (Matthew 5:11)

This blessing extends beyond the present life and into eternal glory. Peter touches on the idea that suffering prepares Christians for future glory. Since Christ suffered and then entered his glory, believers should not think it strange that we too are called to suffer prior to taking our place beside him in heaven. This does not mean that a beleiver becomes worthy through his/her suffering to enter heaven. Rather, since the way to heaven in to follow Jesus Christ, we must first be prepared to follow him in his humiliation if we are afterwards to enter his glory. Peter tells us:

> But rejoice in the degree that you have shared in the sufferings of Christ, so that when his glory is revealed you may also rejoice and be glad. (1 Peter 4:13) (See also 1:3–4 and 5:1.)

For Peter, Christian suffering is only for "a little while" (1 Peter 5:10). He wants us to see the bigger picture, that we are those who will share "in the glory that is to be revealed" (1 Peter 5:1). Paul similarly encourages us to look forward to coming glory when we face troubled times. He writes:

> This momentary affliction is preparing for us an eternal weight of glory beyond all comparison, as we look not to the things that are seen but to the things that are unseen. For the things that are seen are transient, but the things that are unseen are eternal. (2 Corinthians 4:17–18)

Since both in this life and the next, the beleiver is found to be victorious in the face of suffering, the scriptures agree together that we should rejoice in the face of all our trials.

1 Peter 5

Themes in Chapter 5

Chapter 5 begins with brief but important instructions for church leaders/elders. The soberness of the instructions and the greatness of the reward offered for faithful service indicates the importance of their role in God's work. In keeping with his practice throughout this letter, of appealing to Christ's example, Peter again appeals for Christ-like humility among all of God's people. The unity of God's people, and their mutual loving support of each other, is essential if we are to overcome the devil's schemes. The devil prowls around like a hungry lion, but we are able to resist him collectively as we surrender our lives to God. Note that Peter's emphasis is on the church's collective responsibility for its members. We must take care of each other, and exhort each other to submit to God's will, and trust ourselves to his care, if we are to defeat the devil's evil schemes.

Peter returns to the theme of Christian suffering, and again emphasizes that we are all in this together, and that in solidarity we will overcome, provided that our solidarity with other Christians is also solidarity with God.

Peter's final theme, before his personal closing remarks, concerns the glory and power of the Lord Jesus Christ, something which was never far from his mind. Throughout this letter Peter has focused on how Christians are to live whilst anticipating eternal glory.

Verse by Verse

Exhortation to Elders

The word "elder" as used here denotes someone who is part of the leadership of the local church. Although the word can be used of someone older in years, here it is a reference to "their maturity of spiritual experience" (W. E. Vine). The same people are also called "overseers" which indicates the nature of their work. Elders were appointed only if the fulfilled the qualifications outlines in Titus 1:6–9 and 1 Timothy 3:1–7. Whilst originally elders were appointed in the church by the apostles and their co-workers (Titus 1:5), and may today be elected by church ballot, the Scriptures make it clear that elders are called by God and are answerable to him (Acts 20:28). God has given the authority they need to lead his people (Heb 13:7) and in this context God's people should permit themselves to be led (Heb 13:17).

5:1–2 So as your fellow elder and a witness of Christ's sufferings and as one who shares in the glory that will be revealed, I urge the elders among you: Give a shepherd's care to God's flock among you, exercising oversight not merely as a duty but willingly under God's direction, not for shameful profit but eagerly.

Peter considered himself to be an elder, a leader and shepherd of God's Church. He had been an eye witness of Christ's sufferings, death and bodily resurrection (this is the only place in Scripture where we discover Peter had, despite his denial, come close enough to watch his Lord's death). Together with all believers in the Lord Jesus Christ, Peter will share the glory that will be revealed at Christ's coming, when all who believe will be changed into his likeness (1 John 3:2). Peter exhorts his fellow elders to shepherd the flock of God. Peter no doubt understood Paul's comment to the elders of the Ephesian church, that this "flock of God" had been bought by Christ's precious blood (Acts 20:28).

Peter understood that to shepherd God's flock was a call which came to him from the risen Christ: "feed my lamb ... feed my sheep ... take care of my sheep" (John 21:15–17). Christian leaders (elders or pastors) are to nurture, guard, guide and care for God's people.

Nurture

Christian leaders must help other believers to become strong and healthy in their faith. Young converts need to be fed with the sincere milk of the teaching of God's word so that they can mature in faith and in their spiritual experience. Older Christians also need the feeding and encouragement of God's Word. The good elder or pastor will ensure that his congregation is regularly fed with a well-balanced diet of teaching from God's word, never focussing on one favourite teaching, but presenting the whole of the revealed will of God from Scripture (Acts 20:27).

Guard

The shepherd is to protect the flock from wolves – especially those who come dressed in sheep's clothing. These are false teachers (Matt 7:15). They claim to be God's messengers, but are really the servants of Satan, sent to destroy the faith of God's people (2 Cor 11:13–14). A good elder or pastor will seek to keep God's people from error and being led astray by counter-acting false teaching the truth of God's word.

Guide

Elders can show us how to live for God by teaching us God's word. Once again, this is essentially a ministry of the word of God, for that is our guide (Ps 119:105). Christian leaders must break open the truths of God's word and make them accessible to his people, so that we might clearly know the way to live.

Care

Church leaders must show genuine concern and love for all the Christians in their care. They can do so by extending fellowship to all, by being prepared to share their lives with their people and being considerate of their needs. Most especially, this will be through constant prayer for the flock, and by conversation through which leaders can listen out for the needs that people have.

In summary, we see from all these points that an elder's ministry is basically one of preaching, teaching and prayer (Acts 6:2, 4). This is to be, if necessary, to the exclusion of all other matters, which perhaps may be delegated to others.

In addition to all this, elders are to serve as overseers. In doing so, they are serving the Lord Jesus Christ out of love to him (remember how Jesus's call of Peter to be an overseer came with the challenge "do you love me?" in John 21:15–17). As with all our service to God, we must not do things simply because we think it our duty, or as a means to financial gain. We should love our Lord and be willing and eager to serve him.

The AMPNT explains that elders are "not to be dishonestly motivated by the advantages and profits belonging to the office." However, this does not mean that a pastor or elder cannot be paid for fulfilling their ministry. In fact, the practise taught in the NT is that, whenever possible, a minister should be supported financially by the congregation. Why? So that they will be able to devote their full time to the ministry, for the benefit of God's people, rather than to have to work to feed themselves (1 Tim 5:17–18; 1 Cor 9:14). Yet money is never to be the motive of ministry.

5:3 And do not lord it over those entrusted to you, but be examples to the flock.

Elders are not to be overbearing or domineering over those who have been entrusted to their care. They should not enforce their own personal desires or opinions; instead they must exhort and teach according to the word of God. Their lives should be models for other Christians to follow. Peter understands that God has entrusted his people to leaders, those leaders also have authority to carry out that responsibility. Yet such authority must be exercised in humility according to the teaching of Christ (Matt 20:25–28).

5:4 Then when the Chief Shepherd appears, you will receive the crown of glory that never fades away.

Not only are elders to be honoured for their work whilst on earth (e.g. 1 Tim 5:17), but one day, if they have carried out their responsibilities faithfully, they will be rewarded by Christ when he returns (Rev 22:12). The Chief Shepherd (Christ) will give to his faithful co-workers an everlasting crown of glory. Peter's insights into leadership here demonstrate the seriousness of the task entrusted to those who lead. Leadership should never be taken lightly but always in godly obedience.

Humility and the Fight of Faith

5:5 In the same way, you who are younger, be subject to the elders. And all of you, clothe yourselves with humility toward one another, because God opposes the proud but gives grace to the humble.

Just as Peter has exhorted the elders of the church to lead with humility, he now exhorts young people to follow with humility, and a willingness to obey those in authority. All of us should humble ourselves by submitting to and serving each other. The AMPNT says that "God sets himself against the proud. He opposes, frustrates and defeats them, but gives his grace (favour & blessing) to the humble."

5:6–7 And God will exalt you in due time, if you humble yourselves under his mighty hand by casting all your cares on him because he cares for you.

Because of this, we are to humble ourselves ("demote ourselves in our own estimation" AMPNT) under the strong hand of God who can bring things into our lives to humble us and to keep us humble, so that, when we are humble, he will be able to lift us up again and bless us as he longs to do – "in his own good time" (Phillips).

As we humble ourselves in this way, God, who is great and mighty, is more than able to handle all our affairs. So we must cast our cares on him, since after all, he loves and cares for us with a tender care.

5:8–9 Be sober and alert. Your enemy the devil, like a roaring lion, is on the prowl looking for someone to devour. Resist him, strong in your faith, because you know that your brothers and sisters throughout the world are enduring the same kinds of suffering.

We are to be self-controlled and watchful in our Christian walk, being well-balanced and cautious, for we have a very real enemy – the devil. Just like a hungry lion, he hunts his prey and is always on the look-out for an opportunity to devour a believer (by devour, Peter means destroy your faith and your soul).

We are not to take this warning lightly. Peter recalled how once the devil had tried to "sift him as wheat" (Luke 22:31). But we have been given the power of the Holy Spirit, who dwells within us, to overcome Satan. As we withstand the devil by holding fast to our faith in Christ, the devil will flee, for the devil has no answer to

Christ's overwhelming victory (1 John 4:4). Our experiences of being attacked by the devil are not unique to us. It is something that is experienced by every believer, all over the world. But every one of us can know the same victory, because it does not depend on how strong we are, but on the strength of Christ within us.

5:10–11 And, after you have suffered for a little while, the God of all grace who called you to his eternal glory in Christ will himself restore, confirm, strengthen, and establish you. To him belongs the power forever. Amen.

Peter has already explained that God allows trials to come our way to test and strengthen our faith in him. Someone has said that God has put the devil on a leash and this is correct for we understand from Job 1:12 that God – who is sovereign and almighty -- is completely in control of every situation. That is why we can fully trust in him. God only allows trials to come to make us stronger and fully assured in him (Rom 5:3–5). When this purpose has been achieved, he will remove the trial that he was using to do this work in us, since he knows it is no longer needed. Peter here refers to God as the God of all grace who has saved us and called us to share in his eternal glory. Through suffering and difficulties, he is continuing his work of grace within us and he will complete it. So, for this wonderful eternal salvation, we ascribe to him alone glory and dominion forever. Amen.

Closing Remarks

5:12 Through Silvanus, whom I know to be a faithful brother, I have written to you briefly, in order to encourage you and testify that this is the true grace of God. Stand fast in it.

Peter dictated this letter, and it was written by his amanuensis Silas, who at one time had been a companion of Paul (Acts 15:40). Peter regards him as a faithful brother, particularly in his ministry to the church. Peter wrote his letter to confirm that the gospel message which has been preached to us, which we have believed, is the truth concerning the grace of God, which saves us and enables us to stand and continue in the faith.

5:13–14 The church in Babylon, chosen together with you, greets you, and so does Mark, my son. Greet one another with a loving kiss. Peace to all of you who are in Christ.

Peter conveys greetings to his readers from the local church and from Mark, who may have been either his spiritual or natural son. We are to greet one another with a loving display of affection, in Peter's culture, this would be a kiss. Peter's final greeting is "peace," that is, peace with God and the peace of God, which is ours through the death and resurrection of Jesus Christ.

Discussion Questions for Chapter 5

1. In what ways should Christian elders care for God's people?

2. What rewards are promised to those who carry out their responsibility as elders properly?

3. How can we resist and overcome the devil?

4. Discuss what Peter means when he says God will "restore, confirm, strengthen, and establish you."

Going Deeper

Peter's instructions to the elders who shepherd the flock of God in 1 Peter 5:1–4 are surprisingly brief, yet they set out some important principles for all church leaders.

Firstly, Peter recognises that the church belongs to God. The picture of elders shepherding "God's flock," may at first convey the meaning that elders have been entrusted with a duty of care for someone else's property (sheep). But this would be to take Peter's analogy too far. Elders are entrusted with the care of family members, not property—albeit we too are part of the same family. God is our Father, and we are to show our Father's care for younger or weaker relatives in the family.

Secondly, Peter recognises that if elders are shepherds, then they are under-shepherds. The flock of God already has a shepherd, whom Peter refers to (5:4) as "the Great Shepherd." Thus, the responsibility of looking after God's people is not something leaders carry on their own. They work with Jesus Christ to promote his aims and objectives among God's people. In this way, they are not to dominate the flock (5:3), for God does not intend that they should promote their own position or agenda, but Christ's Lordship. The best way they can do this, notes Peter, is to set an example—yielding to Christ's Lordship themselves.

Thirdly, by "shepherding" Peter means to "exercise oversight" (NET), which involves providing guidance in God's will. Chiefly, this will come through godly example and by godly teaching. Elders must show believers how to live for Christ before they can teach believers how to live for Christ. The Bible is the source of guidance for all God's people, and so the ministry of elders is chiefly one of providing biblical teaching (Paul) but it can also extend to rebuke and correction—provided the source of rebuke is, again, the scriptures. There is no sense given in the New Testament that church elders can rebuke, guide or instruct God's people according to their own thoughts and plans.

I have heard some sorry stories of church leaders who have tried to compel members to follow their own instructions—even going so far as telling them whom they may or may not be friends with! I have always taken the line that this is completely unacceptable. As a church leader myself, I see it as my responsibility to lead God's people to understand and live out God's will, as revealed in the scriptures, and quite often, we find ourselves on a journey together of discovering what that good, pleasing, and perfect will is.

Fourthly, elders are to serve willingly, not by compulsion, and not for money. Being an elder/overseer church elder is not a "job," at least not in the modern sense. Leaders must be called and chosen by God, before they can apply for the role! Evidently, they must fulfil the conditions laid down in 1 Tim 3 although Peter overlooks these here. Why? Perhaps in Peter's Jewish congregations, God's moral standards were well known, which they were not in Paul's Gentile congregations. They must also be accepted by, not imposed upon, the churches they serve (a principle found in Acts 2 and 4).

Having said that the elder's motive should not be money, the Bible gives clear instructions that those who feed God's flock should be financially rewarded for this labor, just like artisans are paid for any other service (e.g. 1 Cor 9:714; 1 Tim 5:7). One of the failures of the modern church has been, in my view, to provide its ministers with an adequate living and as a result, just as in the days of Nehemiah (Neh 13:10), the God-called leaders have had to leave to find secular work to feed their families, and the work of God lies in ruins, and wolves are quick to take advantage of the unprotected flock. We must never use Peter's call for elders not to serve for money as an excuse to neglect the equally clear scriptural commands for God's people to support their ministers (see Deut 12:19).

Finally, Peter makes clear that the work of faithful elders will be greatly rewarded when Jesus Christ comes again. They will receive "the crown of glory that never fades away" (5:4). How this will occur is not clear here. However, it represents the Lord's approval for service offered to him, and ultimately that is all any Christian should desire (see also Matt 25:21).

Sample Answers to Discussion Questions

These answers are not necessarily the only "correct" answers to the questions given but are intended to help and guide you in your study.

Chapter 1

1. Since Christians are born of God, their home is in God's presence. This world is not our permanent home, and so we are like pilgrims passing through it on our way to heaven.

2. God has: chosen us, sanctified us, redeemed us, cleansed us from sin, given us peace, given us new birth, given us eternal hope and prepared a place in glory for us. He is keeping us safe by his power.

3. Our trials will prove that our faith is genuine, and as a result God will be glorified.

4. Christians should be reverent, self-controlled and serious about their relationship with God.

Chapter 2

1. Just as babies need milk to grow, so Christians grow through the teaching of the word of God. It reveals to us what God is like and what he requires of us.

2. In the Old Testament, the people gave offerings to God in the temple, through the intermediary of priests, who approached God on their behalf. Believers today ay approach God freely anywhere and at any time (we are like priests). He dwells within us (we are like the temple) and we offer prayers, praise, and our own lives (sacrifices).

3. The beleiver must show God has called them out of darkness by living in the light, being characterised by humility and love, without envy and malice.

4. Peter is paraphrasing Isaiah 53 and applying it to Jesus. He died for us to bring us back – like lost sheep – to God.

Chapter 3

1. As Christians, we submit ourselves to Christ, but this is not a sign of our weakness, but the secret of our strength. A Christian woman who submits to her husband shows her unselfish strength by putting the needs of others first, as Jesus Christ did.

2. Since believers are equal heirs of God in Christ, the husband can defer to his wife in matters such as prayer, realising that her prayers may be as or more effective than his, or that his prayers are less effective without her support.

3. Having compassion will lead us to being patient with others' failings, and perhaps being courteous will help others be more patient with us. Controlling what we say, and being respectful, will prevent many of the problems that can arise in church life.

4. All Christians are called to follow Jesus who suffered and joining with Christ in his suffering is an essential part of our discipleship.

Chapter 4

1. Christ was willing to accept God's will even when it was not pleasant. He remained faithful to God even when this brought opposition.

2. I think unbelievers react negatively to the way our lives have changes because it convicts them of their own need to change, and they do not want to.

3. Using our gifts glorifies the God who gave them, helps others who need them. We will be responsible to God for using the gifts he has given us in this way.

4. Even though we suffer, God will help us in trouble and one day we will be at rest and free from trouble forever.

Chapter 5

1. Christian elders should take God's people on their hearts, teaching and directing them from his word and setting an example by obeying his word themselves.

2. They have the right to expect material support now, but their reward will be entering the joy and glory of the Lord in eternity.

3. We can resist the devil by standing firm in the Christian faith, submitting ourselves to God's will.

4. Through trouble, God will make us stronger, reassuring us by our experience that he will never leave or fail us. As time goes on and more troubles pass our way, the more we will know that next time we face trouble he will be there for us again and bring us through.

Bibliography

1.   *The Amplified New Testament.* Michigan, 1987. Zondervan.

2.   Vine, W.E. *Expository Dictionary of New Testament Words.* London. 1940. Marshall, Morgan & Scott.

3.   Ellicott, Charles John. 1971. *Ellicott's Bible Commentary In One Volume.* London: Pickering & Inglis Ltd.

4.   The Living Bible. 1974. Tyndale.

5.   Matthew Henry Complete Commentary. London. 1960. Marshall, Morgan & Scott.

6.   Wayne Grudem, *1 Peter,* Tyndale New Testament Commentaries (Leicester: IVP, 1988; reprinted 1999)

7.   Peter H. Davids, *The First Epistle of Peter,* New International Commentary on the New Testament (Grand Rapids: Eerdmans, 1995)

8.   1 Peter (Reformed Expository Commentary) Hardcover – 21 Nov 2014 by Daniel M. Doriani Presbyterian and Reformed; First edition (21 Nov. 2014) Philipsburg, NJ

Appendix – How to Use this Study Guide

Good Bible study takes time. Set aside a sufficient time to study the chapter on your own—or divide the chapter into two parts. Allow an hour if possible or at least half an hour for your study.

We recommend that you photocopy the discussion questions (or print them from www.biblestudiesonline.org.uk). Use one for yourself and distribute one each to every member of your study group. Having studied the verses on your own, arrange a meeting so you can join together and compare notes.

Always pray before you begin your study, that God will give you understanding. Then read the chapter itself, from whichever Bible version you prefer. Then sit down, in a quiet place, and read through each verse again together with the guide notes, taking time to reflect and think upon what you read. Make your own notes if possible; recording what God is showing you through the chapter, which might be somewhat different to the guide notes, especially if something is speaking to you personally from a certain verse or chapter. Be sure to share these insights later with your Bible study group. Again, close your study time with a short prayer. Remember that God himself is your greatest teacher, so you need to spend time with him if you wish to understand his word.

We recommend that you concentrate on no more than one chapter at a time. Reading the verses through again will help to ensure that what you have learned will stay in your heart and become part of your life.

Remember—God's word is not an academic textbook to be learned by rote. It is a living word to be hidden in your heart and obeyed in your life. May God bless you as you seek to follow him, employing the best method for spiritual growth which has ever been known to humankind—Bible study!

9 781532 680960